Prin
Charmi
2
Akemi Takaido
Juné

KEI NAGAI
YUASA'S FRIEND. HE'S HAD A CRUSH ON YUASA FROM THE BEGINNING.

YOSHIMI KAGAMI
YUASA'S FRIEND. INTERESTED IN ASAHINA-SENSEI.

Translation	Ken Wakita
Lettering	Zack Giallongo
Graphic Design	Daryl Kuxhouse / Wendy Lee
Editing	Daryl Kuxhouse
Editor in Chief	Fred Lui
Publisher	Hikaru Sasahara

English Edition Published by
DIGITAL MANGA PUBLISHING
A division of DIGITAL MANGA, Inc.
1487 W 178th Street, Suite 300
Gardena, CA 90248

www.dmpbooks.com

First Edition: January 2008
ISBN-10: 1-56970-752-9
ISBN-13: 978-1-56970-752-4

10 9 8 7 6 5 4 3 2 1

Printed in China

MITSURU ASAHINA
HIGH SCHOOL TEACHER. CURRENTLY LIVES WITH YUASA, BUT MAY BE ATTRACTED TO KAGAMI.

HITOSHI YUASA
LIVES WITH ASAHINA-SENSEI, BUT IS NOW CONFUSED AFTER NAGAI CONFESSED HIS FEELINGS TO HIM.

SUMMARY
ASAHINA IS A DELINQUENT TEACHER, WHO OFTEN GOT INTO TROUBLE FOR HIS SEXUAL EXPLOITS. WHEN CONFRONTED BY YUASA ABOUT HIS TRUE ORIENTATION, ASAHINA TRIED TO DENY IT. EVENTUALLY, THE TWO BEGAN A RELATIONSHIP AND CURRENTLY LIVE TOGETHER. MEANWHILE, NAGAI FINALLY CONFESSED HIS FEELINGS TO YUASA, AND KAGAMI BEGAN FLIRTING WITH ASAHINA-SENSEI! CHANGE APPEARS TO BE LOOMING ON THE HORIZON FOR THE RELATIONSHIPS BETWEEN THESE FOUR MEN...

PRINCE CHARMING ⑥

STEP
STEP
STEP
STEP

THERE'S ONLY ONE "L" IN THAT.
パタ
STEP
THANKS.
パタ…
STEP
slide

パーン
SLAP
?
chuckle chuckle
ZZZZZZ
ぐーすか
WHAP
パン
WHAT THE...?!
OH, HEY... GOOD MORNING, MITSURU-CHA --
パンパンパーン
WHAP
WHAP WHAP

HEY! THAT WAS *FAST*...

YOU SKIPPED OUT OF PICKING UP THE CLASSROOM, DIDN'T YOU?
that's low, man.
hell, yes!
LATER.
YEAH.
goodbye!
CAN'T WE GO BACK TO BEING FRIENDS ...?
NOTHING'S CHANGED SINCE THEN...
DON'T WORRY... I UNDERSTAND.
HEY, WHERE'S NAGAI?

HE SPLIT.
WHAT? DID HE SAY HE WAS GOING TO PRACTICE?
UH, NO... BUT DOESN'T HE *ALWAYS* GO THERE?
HE'S BEEN DITCHING PRACTICE LATELY, SO I CAME TO DRAG HIM THERE.
damn...
DITCHING...?! WHY?
I DON'T KNOW WHY... BUT HE'D BETTER START SHOWING UP, OR THEY'RE GONNA KICK HIM OFF THE TEAM...
sheesh!
NAGAI...
I WONDER WHAT'S UP WITH HIM...?
SHWEE
SHOULD I GIVE HIM A CALL?
splash
HEY, COFFEE.

...
UMM...
IT'S GREAT THAT YOU'RE GETTING USED TO ME BEING HERE, BUT...
I'M STARTING TO FEEL MORE LIKE YOUR BUTLER.
BOOM
YEP.
WHAT DO YOU MEAN "YEP" ?
SCREECH
a... are you all right?
but...
who'd want to target you...?
HEY... I'M WATCHING TV.
what's that?!
aaargh!!
CCCCK
TURN IT OFF. THE LAWYER DID IT.
BUT HE HAS AN ALIBI.

YOU KNOW HOW THESE SHOWS ARE... IT'S ALWAYS THE VICTIM WHO GOT AWAY WITH A MINOR INJURY.
AH, THE OLD MISDIRECTION ROUTINE -- PFFT! WHAT A GYP!
SENSEI, IF YOU CAN'T FIGURE OUT THESE STORIES...
YOU MUST BE NAIVE...
CLONK
OUCH!
ROLL
MMM...

AH...
LICK
LICK
HEY...
SENSEI...
WHY DON'T *YOU*...
PUT IT IN THIS TIME...?
K...
HAH...
A... AH...
AH...

IT'S IN.
NN...
K...
WHAT A VIEW...
HAH ...
AH...
ちゅっ
kiss
AHH...
C'MON...
AH...
SENSEI, START MOVING...

NN.
HAH
HAH
A...
AH.

GULP
IT'S COLD.
HEY...
HM?
HOW MANY GUYS DID YOU SLEEP WITH BEFORE ME?
...

WHY DO YOU ASK?
YOU WERE MY FIRST.
HEY, HOLD ON!
HOW CAN I TELL...
IF YOU WERE GOOD OR NOT IF I DON'T COMPARE YOU WITH SOMEONE ELSE?
I'M WORRIED ABOUT WHAT YOU'RE GOING TO SAY RIGHT NOW...
...
LOOK... YOU CAN'T GO OUT THERE HOOKING UP WITH GUYS LIKE YOU DID WITH GIRLS...
IT'S DANGEROUS!
SEE... WITH GIRLS, THEY WERE THE ONES MOST AT RISK...
BUT THE TABLES HAVE TURNED, SO --
CONFUSED

THE WORLD IS FULL OF DANGER!!
SO IT'S OKAY IF IT'S WITH SOMEBODY I ALREADY KNOW?
...
...
SENSEI...
DO YOU... HAVE SOMEONE IN MIND ...?

...YOU'RE AT MISTER BAMBINO'S?
ドッカ
TMP
ドッカ
TMP
I'LL BE RIGHT THERE... NO, I'LL COME THERE...
STAY THERE!
HEY, YUASA! ♡
SO I HEARD YOU'RE LIVING WITH SOMEBODY?
IT SOUNDS NICE, DOESN'T IT? BUT REALITY'S A DIFFERENT STORY.

HUH...?
HEY *NEE-SAN*, HAVE YOU SEEN *KAGAMI*?
YEAH, HE'S IN BACK.
SAY, DID SOMETHING HAPPEN TO NAGAI AT SCHOOL?
WHY DO YOU ASK?
IT'S JUST THAT HE'S... PRETTY *AGGRESSIVE* THESE DAYS.
I DID IT WITH HIM YESTERDAY.
WHA ...?!
I WAS JUST KIDDING AROUND LIKE USUAL, TRYING TO HOOK UP WITH HIM...
AND HE SAID "OKAY" JUST LIKE THAT.
...
I *HEARD* HE WAS GOING OUT WITH THAT RED-HEADED SHORTY -- WAS I WRONG?
RUMOR HAS IT HE'S BEEN SCREWING *EVERYBODY* LATELY.

WELL, HE *IS* RANKED NUMBER ONE ON BAMBINO'S "TO DO" LIST...

SO I'M SURE HE DOESN'T HAVE TROUBLE FINDING PARTNERS.

there's a list?

I'M SORRY...

I SHOULD'VE KNOWN...

YOU COULDN'T HANDLE WHAT I TOLD YOU.

YOU DON'T HAVE TO TROUBLE YOURSELF ANYMORE.

later.

yeah.

IS NAGAI...
HERE TODAY?

HMM... NOPE, HAVEN'T SEEN HIM.

YO.
...
...
SO... WANT TO STRANGLE ME?
NO SECRETS BETWEEN YOU TWO? WHAT A GREAT RELATIONSHIP YOU HAVE.
CHEW CHEW
HE TOLD ME EVERYTHING. YOU GUYS KISSED?
ahm...

...
ALL RIGHT, ALL RIGHT!
IT JUST HAPPENED. THERE'S NOTHING TO IT -- I SWEAR!
WELL... THANKS FOR RESCUING HIM.
I appreciate it.
...
HEH
DON'T MENTION IT.
ANYWAY...
WHAT?
...
WHAT'S UP...?
SENSEI'S BEEN SAYING THINGS LATELY...

I'M NOT SURE ABOUT WANTING TO SLEEP AROUND, BUT...
I DON'T SEE WHY I SHOULD HOLD BACK IF I WANT TO DO IT.
YOU DON'T?
WHAT ABOUT THE FACT THAT OUR RELATIONSHIP IS ILLEGAL?
禁 AGAINST THE LAW 断
CHER
STUDENT
I KNEW YOU LACKED MORALS, BUT...
I never knew you were that depraved.
BOP
WHAT ABOUT YOUR LACK OF MORALS?
YOU DON'T LIKE THE IDEA?
HELL, NO!
JEALOUS?
HELL, YES!
...
WHAT ABOUT A THREE-SOME?

3P
WHA?
WHA?
come again?
WHAT A GREAT IDEA!
IT'S NOT A JOKE.
I'M BEING SERIOUS.
THAT'S WHAT I THOUGHT.
SIGH...
HEH
I KNOW HOW YOU FEEL.
HOW SHOULD I SAY THIS...? HE'S...
UNSTABLE.

THE SIGHT OF HIM WORRIES ME...
I'M THE ONE WHO SHOULD BE WORRIED.
AFTER ALL, I GAVE HIM THE FINAL PUSH...
I know you can't cum...
fucking girls!...
IT'S ALL FOR NOTHING...
IF HE ISN'T SATISFIED WITH HIS NEW LIFE.

AT LEAST THAT'S WHAT'S BEEN RUNNING THROUGH MY HEAD LATELY...
I'M AFRAID HE'S HEADED OUT-OF-CONTROL.
what about a three-some?
hina-chan, you rock!
WELL, IF YOU EVER WANT ME, JUST COME A-KNOCKIN' ♡
ガタ
CREAK
DO YOU EVER SAY "NO"?
you'll fuck anyone.
REJECTING PEOPLE IS TOO DIFFICULT.
SIGH...
OH... YUASA...?
WHAT?
GIVE THIS TO SENSEI FOR ME.
smack
IN YOUR DREAMS.

SEXY THOUGHTS
LOVE
I'LL BE DREAMING ABOUT THAT...
ALL ALONE TONIGHT?
HEY.
WHERE'S YOUR BUDDIES?
OH, RIGHT -- NAGAI...
creak
ガタ..

HE'S NOT...
YOUR BOYFRIEND IS HE?
...
DON'T SCARE ME LIKE THAT.
CATCH YOU LATER.
ガサ
rushe

WHAT'S UP?
ONE OF YOUR TEAMMATES SAID YOU'VE BEEN DITCHING PRACTICE...
AND YOU COULD BE KICKED OFF THE TEAM.
CLICK
FSH
FUCK OFF.
WHAT ...?!
I SAID, FUCK OFF.
...
I CAN'T DO THAT.

...
NAGAI
...?
ギゅ
TMP

YUASA...
I...

I LOVE YOU...
END

PRINCE CHARMING ⑦

MM...
HAAH HAAH...
NAGAI...
HEY.
STOP... IT...

I SAID, CUT IT OUT!!
HA HA HA
FWIP
!!
YOU'RE KIDDING?
I TOLD YOU ALREADY. YOU NEVER LISTEN TO ME...

I'M SORRY...
I'VE NEVER BEEN IN LOVE BEFORE.
THAT MEANS I'VE NEVER SLEPT WITH ANYONE...
I TRULY LOVED WITH ALL MY HEART.

GRAB
WHAT...?
COME WITH ME!

WHAT'S THIS ALL ABOUT?
I DON'T KNOW, MAN...
I HAVE NO IDEA WHAT TO DO.
SO WHY DID YOU BRING ME HERE?
I CAN'T READ YOUR MIND!
QUIET! I TOLD YOU ABOUT EN-CHAN, RIGHT?
WHO ...?

MY CLASSMATE FROM MIDDLE SCHOOL!
EASY! YOU NEVER TOLD ME HIS NAME.
LIKE I SAID...
WE FUCKED LIKE MONKEYS, LIKE IT WAS A GAME...
WE LOVED EACH OTHER, BUT...
LOOKING BACK, IT WAS MORE LUST AND THE EXCITEMENT OF EXPERIMENTATION THAT DID IT FOR US.
YOU THINK MY FEELINGS ARE LUST?
...
NO... WELL... I DON'T KNOW.
I TOLD YOU I WAS NEVER TROUBLED BY MY ORIENTATION LIKE YOU OR SENSEI...

I DO LOVE YOU...
heh...
PROBABLY EVEN MORE THAN I LOVED EN-CHAN.
I KNOW WHO I LOVE AT FIRST SIGHT.
SAME HERE...
BUT I GUESS MY FEELINGS ARE DIFFERENT FROM YOURS.
...

SO... I...
I CAN'T JUST STAND BY WHILE YOU QUIT SOCCER AND GET DRAGGED DOWN THE *SHITHOLE*...
LIKE YOU'RE DOING RIGHT NOW.
shit-hole...
heh...
AH, FORGET IT. I'M NOT ONE TO THINK ABOUT THINGS TOO MUCH.

SO THIS IS YOUR SOLUTION...
IT'S SO LIKE YOU.
FWAP
THIS MAY NOT BE THE RIGHT ANSWER...
WE'RE PROBABLY CROSSING A LINE...
I MAY END UP LOSING YOU...

BUT...
THERE'S NO TURNING BACK NOW.
CREAK
HEY...
AAH...!
I'M FINE...
haah
haah

SIGH
mm?

DO YOU KNOW...
WHAT YOU JUST DID?
YOU LET ME TAKE ADVANTAGE...
OF YOUR KINDNESS...
AND I'M NEVER LETTING YOU GO.

BEEP
BEEP
BEEP
FUMBLE
...
BEEP
BEEP
BEEP
BEEP

WHY DID HE LEAVE THIS HERE...?!
BEEP
BEEP
DESTROY
BEEP
加賀見 好
YOSHIMI KAGAMI
BEEP
BEEP
OH, HEY! YOU FINALLY ANSWERED.
SHUT UP! HE'S NOT HERE...!
SENSEI ...?
HUH? WHERE'S THE PHONE AT?
RIGHT HERE.
AT SENSEI'S PLACE? DID HE FORGET TO RECHARGE IT?
why have a cell phone?

SORRY FOR WAKING YOU SENSEI...
HE WAS *HERE* JUST A MOMENT AGO.
NO ANSWER FROM NAGAI-KUN, EITHER.
did they leave?
HICCUP
WE WE'RE WONDERING IF THEY WANTED TO GO HAVE BREAKFAST.
IT'S 4 AM!
...
THAT'S MORNING, ISN'T IT?
I DON'T KNOW HOW YOU GUYS HAVE THE ENERGY TO MAKE IT TO SCHOOL EVERY DAY.
OH... SORRY FOR BOTHERING YOU SENSEI.
WELL, I WON'T KEEP YOU ANY LONGER. GO BACK TO SLEEP --
OH, SENSEI... DID I HEAR YOU SAY YOU WANTED TO DO IT WITH ME?
...
ARE YOU IN BED?
HUH? WELL... YEAH.

SEN-SEI ♡
YEAH...?
DOES IT FEEL GOOD?
HUH?
DID YOU DROP YOUR PANTS ON THE FLOOR?
YEAH, RIGHT THERE...
SMOOTH BUT GENTLE... YEAH, STROKE IT...
HEY...
ARE YOU GETTING TURNED ON...?
HEY ...!
AH...
I'M... GETTING TURNED ON, TOO...
HAAH HAAH...
UNN...
I'M HANGING UP NOW.

HM? NOT WORKING? I USED TO BE A PART-TIME PHONE SEX OPERATOR, AND I WAS PRETTY GOOD...
MAYBE SENSEI'S MORE INCLINED TOWARD S&M?
HOW THE HECK DO YOU DO **BONDAGE** OVER THE PHONE?
scratch
scratch
ボリ
ボリ
MANY MASOCHISTS ARE TURNED ON BY WORDS...
THERE'S EVEN A "HOW TO" MANUAL.
A MANUAL?
...
YEP! FOR EXAMPLE, IF THE PERSON STARTS GETTING HORNY, YOU REPLY WITH AN INSULT TO SETTTLE THEM DOWN.
REALLY ...?
HM? ARE YOU INTERESTED?
I'M NOT A MASOCHIST, THOUGH.
HA HA
YEAH, THAT'S TRUE.

YOSHI ♡
C'MON!
I'M HUNGRY, TOO... LET ME TAG ALONG!
what?!
c'mon let's drink some more!
HICCUP
all right, all right!
oh, geez! please don't come.
YOSHI?
YOU'RE MORE LIKE A SADIST WHO GIVES OUT ABUSE.
YOSHIMI-CHAN.
WHENEVER YOU'RE ALONE AND FEELING LONELY, FEEL FREE TO GIVE ME A CALL ♡
YOSHI, C'MON!
HEY... I SAID I'M COMING --
BEEEEEEP
...
PLIP
...

パタ
STEP
パタ
STEP
THERE YOU ARE. WHEN DID YOU GET BACK?
HUH ...?
ふあ～
YAWN
I SLEPT HERE BECAUSE I DIDN'T WANT TO WAKE YOU...
...
WHAT?
HUH...?

OH... IT'S NOTHING.
WAIT! HOLY SHIT... WHAT TIME IS IT?!
SENSEI WOKE UP ON HIS OWN? IT MUST BE LATE!
わたわた
rustle rustle

good morning.

good morning.
HEY. YOU'RE LATE.
hey.
YEAH... I DIDN'T GET MUCH SLEEP.
how's it going?
SO, HOW WAS IT?
HOW WAS *WHAT*?
I SAW YOU TWO COMING OUT OF THE HOTEL.
...
OH, SHIT! YOU THOUGHT I WAS *SERIOUS*?
YOU...!
was only kidding
fell for it

DON'T TRY AND **START** ANYTHING.
HMM ...?
I SEE...
HEY, IF I HAVE FEELINGS...
I SHOULD DO SOMETHING ABOUT THEM, RIGHT?
HEH
FEELINGS?
whose feelings?
my feelings. mine.
my heart beats, too
trust me.

KNOCK
KNOCK
KERCHAK
YES?
HI, I'M LOOKING FOR KOMORI-SENSEI.
HMM...
he might be in the faculty room.

KACHAK
STEP
SENSEI? HAVE YOU SEEN KOMORI-CHAN?
NOPE... WHAT, DID HE FIND OUT ABOUT YOUR *BIKE* AGAIN?
GIVE THE GUY A BREAK, EH? HE'S JUST WORRIED ABOUT YOU.
YEAH, AND I'M THE TYPE THAT *LIKES* TO MAKE HIM WORRY.
HE WAS MY TEACHER IN FIRST YEAR...
AND I'VE BEEN HITTING ON HIM EVER SINCE... BUT HE DOESN'T TAKE ME SERIOUSLY.
thump
WELL, *DUH*.

WHY? IS IT THE TEACHER-STUDENT THING?
creak
creak
ガタ
ガタ
chak
パタ
HOW ABOUT YOU, ASAHINA-SENSEI?
SQUEAK
キュル…
MOVE.
FWAP
パタ…

RUB
SENSEI...
...

YOU WANT ME, DON'T YOU?
I WANT YOU, TOO... C'MON, LET'S DO IT.

YOU'RE EXACTLY LIKE YUASA TOLD ME YOU'D BE.
...
HMM?
do you... have someone in mind?
SENSEI, LET ME TELL YOU...
THE MINUTE YOU GAVE HIM THE "OK" SIGN, THAT SEALED IT-- HE'LL KEEP COMING AFTER YOU LIKE YOU ALREADY SLEPT WITH HIM.
GRIP
CHUCKLE ...
that bastard.
no denial.
THUMP
...

YOU DIDN'T *HIT* ME THIS TIME.
HUH?
GUESS THAT MEANS YOU'RE NOT PISSED OFF?

カチャ
KERCHAK
...
パタ
SLAM
AW, MAN...! I'LL GO STRAIGHTEN IT OUT.
HOW ...?
I'LL SAY THERE WAS SOMETHING IN YOUR CONTACTS.
WHAT-EVER...
HEH
パタ
KACHAK

LOVE...
AND PASSION...
SWAYS...
THEIR HEARTS.
END

PRINCE CHARMING ⑧

HAAH
HAAH
SIGH
DIDN'T YOU SAY...
YOUR FAMILY'S IN THE LIVING ROOM DOWN-STAIRS?
DON'T WORRY, THE DOOR'S LOCKED.
THAT'S NOT WHAT I MEANT...

AH...
ぶしっ
ACHOO
ぶしっ
ACHOO
HM? AM I CATCHING A COLD?
SNIFFLE
WHERE'S MY SHIRT...?
BY THE WAY... WHY'D I COME HERE...? OH, YEAH -- THE NOTES...
AND THE VIDEO.
RIGHT... THE GAME I MISSED LAST WEEK...
NNG
くちゅ
smack

H...
SMOOCH
ぐいっ
SHOVE
HEY...
DON'T BE... SO AGGRESSIVE.
haah haah
I'M STILL NOT SATISFIED...
MM.

COUGH
COUGH
QUIET...
SORRY... SHIT... I THINK I REALLY ***HAVE*** GOT A COLD!
WHERE ARE YOU GOING...?
I DON'T WANT TO GIVE IT TO YOU, SO I'LL SLEEP ON THE COUCH...
ゴホッ
COUGH
DON'T WORRY ABOUT IT. ***I'M*** THE ONE WHO'LL HAVE TO SUFFER LOOKING AFTER YOU IF YOU GET SICK.
WHAT?
OH, SO SENSEI IS KIND TO SICK PEOPLE, EH?
ペ
KICK
hey! it was a compli-ment!
WELL, MY PARENTS ARE THE SAME WAY.
...
TAP TAP
WHAT...?

BY THE WAY, WHAT DID YOU TELL YOUR PARENTS ABOUT MOVING?
ISN'T IT A BIT LATE TO DISCUSS THAT ...?
I DIDN'T THINK OF IT UNTIL NOW.
it's been several weeks since they started living together
huh?
NOTHING, REALLY. MY PARENTS ARE PRETTY LIBERAL... THEY'VE ALWAYS LET ME STAY OUT. BESIDES, I'VE GOT A LOT OF BROTHERS...
SO THEY MAY NOT HAVE EVEN NOTICED I'M GONE.
I'M THE YOUNGEST OF THE SIX, SO...
SIX?!
COUGH
YOU'VE GOT TO BE KIDDING...
really?
YOUR PARENTS HAD SIX KIDS IN THIS DAY AND AGE?
YOU'RE THE ONLY PERSON I'VE EVER MET FROM A FAMILY WITH SIX KIDS!
HEY, I TAKE THAT AS AN INSULT! MY FAMILY'S KNOWN AS BEING FRIENDLY AND OUTGOING...
why are you getting so excited?

DO THEY ALL LOOK LIKE YOU...?
HUH?
YOUR BRO-THERS.
what's the big deal?
KINDA.
chuckle
inaccurate notion
it's sextup-lets!
HA HA HA...
WAS IT THAT FUNNY?
chuckle
chuckle
WHAT THE HECK...? I CAN'T STOP LAUGHING...
BWA HA HA HA
I UNDERSTAND. IT'S THAT TIME LATE AT NIGHT WHEN A PERSON CAN'T CONTROL THEIR LAUGHTER, RIGHT?
SHAKE SHAKE
...
...
SENSEI, YOU'RE PROBABLY AN ONLY CHILD, ARENT YOU?
six... six...
SIGH

SENSEI, WOULD YOU TAKE THIS TO THE LIBRARY...?
OH, AND THIS, TOO.
SOME-THING WRONG?
どッきーん jolt
AH... NO!
UMM... I HAVEN'T *TOLD* ANYONE, SO DON'T BE CONCERNED.
HUH?
LIKE I SAID, I BELIEVE PEOPLE'S *ORIENTATION* SHOULD BE THEIR OWN BUSINESS...
BUT, WELL... MIGHT I SUGGEST YOU HOLD OFF ON SUCH A RELATIONSHIP UNTIL *AFTER* GRADUATION...? BEING TEACHER AND STUDENT AND ALL...
...

I UNDERSTAND THAT YOU AND KAGAMI HAVE ***FEELINGS*** FOR EACH OTHER... I DO...
previously
I'll go straighten it out.
how...?
WHAT DID HE TELL YOU?
DO YOU HAVE A FEVER...?
I'M OKAY. I JUST GOT SOME ASPRIN FROM THE NURSE'S OFFICE, SO IT'S NO BIG DEAL. WHAT'S WRONG...?
HUH?

YOU'VE NEVER STARTED A CONVERSATION WITH ME AT SCHOOL BEFORE.
REALLY ...?
DON'T WORRY.
I WON'T.
HEH
see you later.
yeah.
パ ク
STEP
パ・・ク
STEP

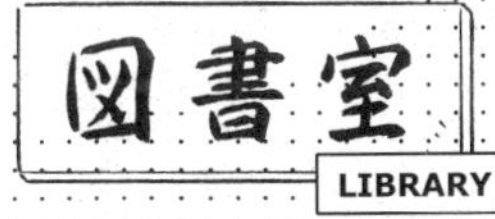

TMP

MMM♡
SENSEI, DO YOU SHOWER EVERY MORNING?
I DON'T HAVE TIME TO SHOWER IN THE MORNING.
HEH
WHAT DO YOU WANT?
OH, NOTHING. JUST WONDERING IF SENSEI WANTED ME FOR SOMETHING. YOU LOOKED AT ME JUST NOW, DIDN'T YOU?
YOU TOLD KOMORI-SENSEI THAT WE'RE GOING OUT.
OH, MAN! THAT'S GOING AROUND *ALREADY*?
NO, KOMORI-SENSEI IS KEEPING IT A SECRET. YOU KNOW HOW HE IS.
TMP
AWW... I SHOULD'VE STARTED THE RUMOR SOMEWHERE ELSE, THEN...
PLAN FAILED

ぺろん
LICK
shiver
ピク
SENSEI... WHAT DO YOU WANT WITH ME AND YUASA?
整理整頓
PLEASE RETURN BOOKS
IF IT'S TWO-ON-ONE, IT MIGHT NOT BE WHAT YOU HAD IN MIND...
YOU COULD BE THE ONLY ONE NAKED...
LEFT TO SHOW YOUR BODY TO US...
FROM TOP TO BOTTOM...
AS WE *TOY* WITH YOU...
GROPE

...AND YOU'RE FORCED TO CUM OVER AND OVER AGAIN...
GKK...
SIGH...
HEY ...!
SHH...! SHH...
DON'T LET HIM SEE US...
FLIP
UNLIKE KOMORI-CHAN, HE WON'T TAKE IT AS A JOKE.
komori didn't take it as a joke.

...
SENSEI?
SENSEI, ARE YOU GOING FOR MY BODY?
ぱっ
grab
NEED ANY HELP?
DON'T MOVE.

I *KNEW* YOU WERE A SADIST, SENSEI...
whoa ♡
THAT'S RIGHT -- YOU SAW ME NAKED ONCE, DIDN'T YOU?
RUB RUB
すり すり
IF YOU LIKED WHAT YOU SAW, ALL YOU HAD TO DO WAS ASK...
...
...
IT'S... GETTING HARDER...
I *AM* A GUY, AFTER ALL.

TURN
BESIDES, IF A GUY AS HOT AS *SENSEI* DOES THAT TO ME...
I CAN'T CONTROL IT.
grasp
YOU'RE SMALLER THAN I THOUGHT.
there!
WHAT THE ...?!
I CAN'T FUCK YOU HERE, SO WE'RE JUST GONNA PRETEND.
LIFT
THRUST

SEE, IT'S IN.
OKAY?
hey...
STOP... THE VICE-PRINCIPAL ...!
ガタ
CREAK
HE'S GONE.
whisper whisper
WHY DIDN'T YOU *TELL* ME?
HUH?
WHY, SO YOU CAN THINK OF OTHER GUYS?

WE'RE PRETENDING MY COCK IS DEEP IN YOUR ASS RIGHT NOW...
GET IT OUT!! BREAK TIME'S ALMOST OVER!

WELL, THAT WAS *SORTA* REAL... I GUESS...

SHALL I EXPLAIN, MY DARLING?
SHUT UP!
UMM...
THUMP THUMP THUMP THUMP
ドキドキドキドキ
AH, FORGET IT.
pretend you didn't see us.
I THINK YOU JUST ACKNOWLEDGED OUR RELATION-SHIP...
ガッ
KICK
CHUCKLE
...

WHAT IS IT? I HAVE TO GO TO WORK.
YOU *LIKE* SENSEI, DON'T YOU?
YES, I DO.
...
YOU'RE JUST PLAYING AROUND.
AND IT'S *FUN*, TOO!
WHAT ABOUT YOU?
は—…
droop
SIIIGH
IT'S OBVIOUS THAT KEI-CHAN'S SERIOUS...
I THOUGHT ONCE HE *TOLD* YOU, YOU WOULDN'T TAKE THINGS ANY FURTHER, BUT...
WHY'D YOU THINK THAT?

WELL...
ザ
RUSTLE
MM-HM... SAME SMELL AS SENSEI.
sniff
WHAT?
ぎゅむ〜
GRAB
WHAT ARE YOU DOING?
you're too close.
SEE? YOU DON'T RESIST MUCH AFTER ALL...
POOR NAGAI.
WHAT DOES *THAT* MEAN?
THE FIRST ONE YOU HIT ON...
HUH...?
THE GUY YOU WENT OUT WITH... WHAT WAS HIS NAME... *ENTANI?*
YOU AND EN-CHAN DIDN'T DECIDE WHO WAS ON TOP OR BOTTOM, DID YOU?
SO?

SO, BASICALLY YOU DON'T HAVE A PREFERENCE.
FOR WHAT?
BEING TOP OR BOTTOM.
OH... NO.
SO DEEP DOWN INSIDE, YOU REALLY DON'T GIVE A DAMN...
IF YOUR PARTNER LOVES YOU FROM THE BOTTOM OF *HIS* HEART, HE CAN FEEL THAT WITHIN YOU.
DON'T LET NAGAI GO TOO FAR, OKAY?
IF YOU THINK YOUR SEX IS CASUAL, YOU'D BETTER BE CAREFUL -- HE DOESN'T FEEL THE SAME WAY.
WHAT ABOUT YOU...?
ME?
YOU ONLY *HAVE* CASUAL SEX!
OH, WELL... THAT'S AS HIGH AS MY SCALE GOES.

YOU WON'T BE ABLE TO MAKE SENSEI HAPPY THAT WAY.
HA HA
WHAT ...?
YOU SAY IT LIKE IT'S GONNA LAST FOREVER.
SIGH ...
Cough
THERE'S SO MUCH GOING ON...
MY HEAD FEELS LIKE IT'S GOING TO EXPLODE...

YUASA!
...
YOU DON'T LOOK WELL...
YEAH... I'M GOING STRAIGHT HOME.
TO SENSEI'S PLACE?
YEAH...
CASUAL...
SEX...

ARE YOU FEELING WORSE?
YEAH... WELCOME HOME.
DID YOU TAKE SOME-THING?
YEAH...

SLIDE ス
DID YOU EAT?
UMM... I GOT SOME UDON ON THE WAY HOME...
WITH SOME SIDES... ENOUGH FOR TWO.
ALL RIGHT. JUST RELAX AND GET SOME SLEEP.
パタ
SHUT
...
WHAT ARE YOU DOING ...?
QUIET. THIS IS JUST A DREAM.

OH. JUST A DREAM...
IT HAS TO BE...
SIGH...
SERIOUSLY...
WHAT *AM* I DOING...?

MM...?
...
LET ME GUESS... HE FELL ASLEEP WHILE CHECKING TO SEE IF I NEEDED A NEW ICE PACK...
yep, gotta be!!
BLIP
BLIP
MAIL FROM:
KEI NAGAI.
HOW'S YOUR COLD?
IF YOU NEED ANYTHING, LET ME KNOW.

LOOKS LIKE MY FEVER'S GONE DOWN.
BUT...
I THINK SOME OF THE FEVER HAD TO DO WITH EVERYTHING GOING THROUGH MY HEAD THESE DAYS.
I DON'T KNOW, MAN...
BLIP
BLIP BLIP
BLIP
...
どっかり
THUD

IT'S ME...
I'M THE CAUSE OF ALL MY TROUBLES...
IT'S ALL MY FAULT.

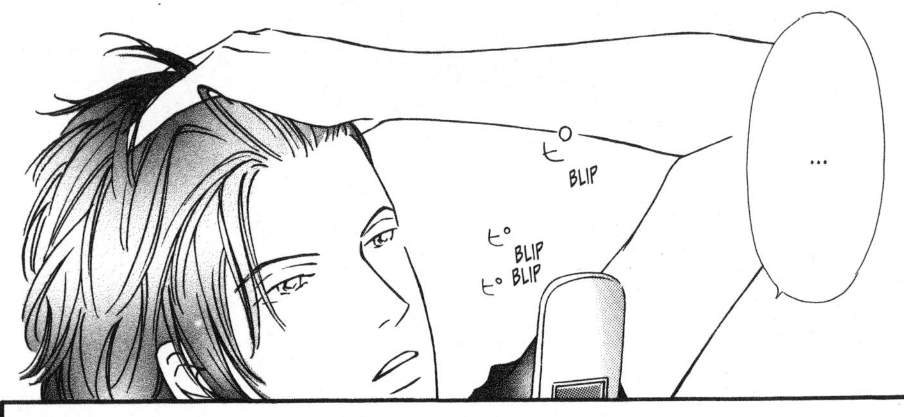
...
ピ BLIP
ピ BLIP
ピ BLIP
ピ BLIP
ピ BLIP
I'D BETTER CHILL OUT...

I NEED TIME TO THINK EVERYTHING OVER, OR I'M GONNA GO NUTS.

damn... what time is it...?
HEY...
WHY DIDN'T YOU WAKE ME...?
BAM

YUASA?

パタ STEP

パタ STEP

HE LEFT ALREADY ...?

MUST BE FEELING BETTER.

パタ STEP

MORNING OF THE FOURTH WEEK LIVING TOGETHER ...

he forgot to take out the trash!

END

PRINCE CHARMING ⑨

WHAT A BEAUTY...
YET HE SEEMS SO FAR AWAY.
IT'S HARD TO THINK THAT I ONCE HELD YOU IN MY ARMS.
キーンコーン
カーンコーン
ring
riiing
stand...
ガタ
ガタ...
GATAK
bow...
I'VE DECIDED TO TAKE SOME TIME OFF...
SO I CAN EXAMINE THINGS BETWEEN US...
BUT I CAN'T SEEM TO SHAKE THIS FEELING --

SMACK
びたーん
WHAT THE HELL IS THIS...?!
SUPPLIES
1. Can openers, kitchen utensils,
I THOUGHT YOU DIDN'T KNOW WHERE EVERYTHING IS YET...?
WHY ARE MY HOUSEHOLD SUPPLIES PUT WHERE *YOU* WANT THEM?!
TRUST ME, IT'LL BE HANDIER ONCE YOU GET USED TO IT.
...
SO...
YOU'RE GOING HOME?
I HAVE THINGS ON MY MIND, SO I AM FOR A WHILE.

STIFLED ANGER
IF YOU'RE GOING, THEN DON'T LEAVE YOUR JUNK AT MY PLACE...!
BUT I GOT MORE STUFF WHILE I WAS THERE...
OH, SPEAKING OF JUNK, DID YOU TAKE OUT THE TRASH? YOU'D BETTER START REMEMBERING...
SHUT UP!
OH, THIS IS GETTING GOOD!
IT IS?
DON'T YOU THINK? REALLY!
WHAT'S UP WITH ASAHINA?
HMM... I THINK THOSE TWO ARE...
what?!
YOU'RE KIDDING...
but yuasa is...
LOOKS LIKE I'D BETTER STEP IN...
oh, and then...
you do it...!!
SEN-SEI!
YOU'RE QUITE ENTHUSIASTIC TODAY AREN'T YOU? ARE YOU DRUNK AGAIN, OR JUST IRRITATED?
HA HA HA HA

ぴゅん
SWISH
パ
FWAP
nice save!
yay!
パチ clap
パチ clap

YOU...! DETENTION OFFICE -- AFTER SCHOOL!
イライラ イライラ
IRK IRK IRK IRK
don't think this is over!
you're abusing your powers, mitsuru-chan...

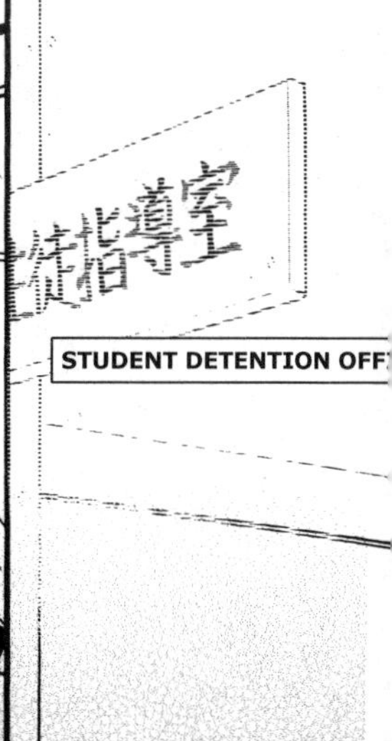
徒指導室
STUDENT DETENTION OFF

...
WHY ARE YOU TWO HERE...?

I THOUGHT IT WOULD BE FUN... ER, I MEAN, *I* DESERVE TO BE SCOLDED BY YOU, TOO.
chomp
chew
HE DRAGGED ME ALONG.
...
SO, HOW ARE THINGS BACK AT HOME? LEAVE FOR A WHILE AND LOSE YOUR PLACE, HM?
SPACE IS TIGHT, I HEAR.
YEAH, MY BED ALREADY BECAME A STORAGE AREA... AND THE TOP OF MY DESK IS COVERED WITH MY SISTER'S BRAS...
WAIT A MINUTE... YOUR SISTER ...?
WHICH ONE?
OR *SISTERS?*
plural?
HEY! I MET ONE OF YOUR BROTHERS THE OTHER DAY. IT WAS SATOSHI-SAN OR ATSUSHI-SAN...
DID HE WEAR A SUIT? THAT'S SATOSHI.
I'm not sure.
HEY...
UM... SO WHAT'S THIS ABOUT?
WHY WE ARE *HERE*...?

THAT'S EASY...
"HOW WILL THIS SEPARATION AFFECT OUR RELATIONSHIP?"
LOOKS LIKE IT ALREADY HAS IN SOME WAYS...
...
AND WE HAVEN'T DECIDED WHEN TO HAVE OUR *THREESOME!*
HEY!
THREESOME?
WHAT KIND OF THREE-SOME?
WHICH?
example:
choose any two you like!
OR WE COULD HAVE A *FOURSOME!*
I *KNEW* YOU WERE GONNA SAY THAT...
...

WAIT A SEC...
WHAT'S ***YOUR*** PART IN ALL THIS...?
I'M SLEEPING WITH YUASA.
COULD YOU SAY IT A LITTLE MORE ***BLUNTLY?***
HE PLAYS SPORTS -- HE'S AGGRESSIVE.
SHUT UP!
コンコン
KNOCK KNOCK
ガラッ
SLIDE
OH, SENSEI! I NEED TO USE THE ROOM... ARE YOU JUST ABOUT FINISHED?
UHH...
komori-chan's fact-check
gay
gay
gay
un-known
seems popular with younger students
added fact
OH... WELL... HAVE FUN...
CREAK
ガタ
wanna join us?

SO, ARE YOU STAYING HOME?
YEAH, I'VE GOTTA GET MY ROOM BACK.
hey...
I'M GOING TO PRACTICE.
later.
HOW ABOUT YOU? GOING TO WORK?
HMM...
HEY!
STOP THE CAR!

...IT'S HIM!
OH, SHIT -- YOU'RE RIGHT!
WAIT, ISN'T THAT ...?
SO... THEY GO TO THIS SCHOOL...
...
YOU KNOW HIM?
NO...
THAT *PUNK* ...!

HUH?
ガタ
ガタ
ガタ
rustle
rustle
WHERE'S THE LETTER OPENER ...?
ガタッ
rustle
ガチャッ
crash
DAMN IT! WHERE THE HELL DID HE PUT MY LETTER OPENER?!
バン
BAM
...
パ
タ
STEP

DING DONG...

STEP パ…タ…

...

THOUGHT YOU MIGHT BE *LONELY*.

AREN'T YOU GOING TO LET ME IN?

I BROUGHT YOU SOME ICE CREAM...

ガサ

rustle

...

YOU THOUGHT...
IT MIGHT BE YUASA, DIDN'T YOU?

...
I NEVER EXPECTED TO SEE YOU SO DOWN.
WHATEVER.
STEP
YOU THOUGHT HE'D NEVER CHOOSE TO LEAVE WITHOUT ASKING YOU FIRST...
ISN'T THAT WHY YOU'RE SO UPSET?
SENSEI, YOU'RE SO CUTE...
YOU MAKE ME *JEALOUS!*
YOU'RE AWFULLY PLEASED WITH YOUR-SELF...
GUESS YOU'RE A PRETTY SICK TWIST, AREN'T YOU?

DEFINITELY.
ずるん
yank
WHA...?!
STOP...
ベ~..
LICK
H...
HEY...
AH...
ヤ...
CHNKK
HUH?

AW, *NUTS*...
HEH
BUMP
YOU BASTARD!
YOU'RE ACTING TOO FAST!
NO ONE KNOWS WHAT TOMORROW MAY BRING, SO I MADE MY MOVE.
YOU COMING *BACK* ALREADY?
lick
I JUST CAME TO PICK UP SOME OF MY STUFF!
CHOMP
hello...?
YES... OH, REALLY? HAPPY BIRTHDAY.
YEAH, I'M HERE WITH YUASA... ALL RIGHT, LATER!

chomp
THEY'RE HAVING A BIRTHDAY PARTY FOR NEE-SAN AT BAMBINO'S TONIGHT... WANNA GO?
SURE.
NAGAI'S THERE, TOO.
OKAY, LET'S GO...
OR, WHILE WE'RE ALL *HERE*, WE COULD TRY THAT THREESOME...
OUT!
YOUR JUNK'S OVER THERE... TAKE IT AND GO.
STEP
WHAT? YOU'RE STILL *MAD* AT ME?
STEP
NAGAI'S WAITING.

IN YOUR DREAMS.
I TAKE IT YOU'RE *JEALOUS?*
HEY...
SO WHAT DID HE DO TO YOU?
C'MON.
YOU'RE THE ONE WHO'S JEALOUS!
GRAB
YOU'RE DAMN *RIGHT* I AM...

MM...
NN...
NNN...
HAAH
HAAH
nn...

ARE YOU LEAVING *ALREADY*, YOSHI?
HICCUP
YEAH, I NEED TO CATCH SOME SLEEP.
good night.
good night.
KER-CHAK
LEAVING SO SOON...?

WHAT'S UP...?

YOU *KNOW* WHAT'S UP.
IT'S SOMEONE *ELSE'S* BIRTHDAY?
WE AREN'T PLAYING GAMES HERE, BOY.

WE KNOW, MAN. THAT HOTTIE... HE'S YOUR TEACHER? GOOD ONE.

...
ぺち
slap
YOU'RE PRETTY SMART.
THAT *TRICK* YOU PLAYED ON US... NOT BAD.

HEH
I'LL BET YOU PEED YOUR PANTS A LITTLE.
HA HA
YEAH... WELL...
I *HATE* FIRES.

ビイイイイ…
SLASH
CAN'T YOU JUST GIVE ME A WARNING, OR SOME-THING...?
AND RISK BEING FUCKED AROUND BY YOU AGAIN?
ガ
THUD

OH, SHIT...
BEEP BEEP BEEP
HEY. I THOUGHT YOU LEFT...?
N...
NAGAI...
KAGAMI?

DING DONG
DING DONG
...
...
HMM...?
WHAT THE FUCK...?
THUD
ガタ
SORRY... I DIDN'T KNOW WHERE ELSE TO GO...

WHAT HAPPENED ...?
THUD
THE HOSPITAL... I'LL CALL AN AMBULANCE...
DON'T! HE'S BEEN STABBED.
TH...
THERE'S NO TIME TO ARGUE...
ガタ
STEP
WHAT'S GOING ON...?
...
WHAT THE...?!
WHO *DID* THIS?!
THERE WAS A DOCTOR AT BAMBINO'S WHO PATCHED HIM UP.
LUCKILY, HE SAID THE WOUND ISN'T AS BAD AS IT LOOKS.

RUSTLE
ガ
NO, I JUST CAME TO PICK UP MY STUFF.
SO... BACK HERE ALREADY?

HEY...!
...
ANY IDEA WHO DID THAT TO HIM?
IT WAS A FIGHT, RIGHT? SOMEONE SHOULD'VE STOPPED IT.
THAT WAS NO FIGHT... A MUGGING, MAYBE.
IT WAS THREE GUYS.

THERE WERE WITNESSES?
NEE-SAN SAW THREE GUYS FOLLOWING KAGAMI AS HE LEFT THE CLUB.
THREE... YOU MEAN...?
YEP, MOST LIKELY.
I'LL BET THEY FOUND OUT ABOUT HIM RESCUING SENSEI.
I KNOW KAGAMI DIDN'T SAY ANYTHING, BUT...
THOSE BASTARDS! NEE-SAN WARNED US THEY WERE A BUNCH OF DICKS...
WHO BRAGGED ABOUT BEING *CRIMINALS!*
IF WE GO TO THE HOSPITAL AND THEY REPORT IT TO THE POLICE...
IT MIGHT COST YOU YOUR JOB, AND GET KAGAMI KICKED OUT OF SCHOOL...
I DIDN'T KNOW THAT...
SORRY... I DIDN'T WANT TO FREAK YOU OUT, AND KAGAMI PROBABLY THOUGHT THE SAME THING.

SIGH
IS HE... GONNA BE ALL RIGHT?
TAP
MM... ACCORDING TO THE DOCTOR, THE REASON THE WOUND'S SO SHALLOW WAS PROBABLY TO INFLICT THE MOST PAIN...
WHILE KEEPING HIM CONSCIOUS...
AS THEY BEAT HIM UP.
BASTARDS...
SENSEI, ARE YOU OKAY?
LET ME DO IT...
CLINK
IT'S ALL MY FAULT.

パタン
SHUT
damn it...
SENSEI...
CLINK CLINK
カタカタ
SO...
I AM AT
SENSEI'S
PLACE...
...
ARE YOU...
ALL RIGHT?
カチャ
CLINK

I'LL BE READY FOR A THREESOME BY TOMORROW.
IT WAS *THOSE* GUYS WHO DID IT, WASN'T IT?
WHY DID YOU...?
DON'T WORRY.
HUH?
THEY WERE... PISSED OFF THAT I FUCKED THEM AROUND BY STARTING THAT FIRE...
THEY'RE A BUNCH OF IDIOTS, SO I'M SURE THEY WON'T COME AFTER YOU, SENSEI...
WHAT...
ARE YOU SAYING...?

MM?
WHY DO YOU AND YUASA...
WHY DO YOU WANT TO PROTECT ME?
BECAUSE I LOVE YOU.
IT'S ANNOYING!

WHY DOES HE HAVE TO SAY IT NOW?
nice one, saying it when you're at your weakest.
YEAH, THAT'S GOTTA BE A NEW LOW.
purr ゴロ
purr ゴロ
purr ゴロ
...
END

PRINCE CHARMING 10

LOOKS LIKE YOUR WOUND'S HEALING.
HOW'S THE PAIN?
HURTS A LITTLE WHEN I LAUGH.
ARE YOU SURE? I STILL THINK YOU SHOULD GO TO THE HOSPITAL...
NO "GET WELL" KISS TODAY...?
WHEN DID I EVER GIVE YOU ONE?
OH? MAYBE I DREAMT IT, THEN.
I COULD'VE SWORN I SMELLED YOU WHEN I WAS ALSEEP IN YOUR BED...

パコーン
CLONK
YOU'VE GOT SOME NERVE SAYING THAT IN FRONT OF ME!
WHY ARE YOU HERE? I THOUGHT YOU LEFT?
RIGHT! WITH YOU AROUND, WHO KNOWS WHAT COULD HAPPEN?
CUDDLE
CUDDLE
YOU'RE JUST THE HOUSEKEEPER, BUT I'M THE SPECIAL GUEST!
SENSEI SAYS HE'S GONNA LOOK AFTER ME...
BASH
YOU SEEM TO HAVE REGAINED YOUR HEALTH.

WHAT...?!
THE DOOR WAS OPEN.
OH, I MUST'VE LEFT IT --
CLONK
HERE'S YOUR STUFF.
OH, THANKS.
THUD
WHAT'S THAT?
THE THINGS I LEFT AT SCHOOL...
HUH?
IT'S ALMOST SUMMER BREAK.
CAN'T GO BACK TO SCHOOL LIKE *THIS*, CAN I?
THOSE YOUR OLD GLASSES?
YEP. WERE THEY IN MY LOCKER?
DO YOU HAVE TO BRING YOUR STUFF HERE? I JUST GOT RID OF *HIS* JUNK...
OH, I'VE DECIDED TO COME BACK...
so I'm bringing it again.
...
YOU ALL RIGHT?
YEAH. THANKS FOR EVERYTHING.
NEE-SAN AND EVERYONE ARE WORRIED. YOU SHOULD GIVE THEM A CALL.

IT'S TOO DANGEROUS. I'LL BRING IT OVER.
THERE'S LOTS OF PARKING HERE AT THE APART-MENTS, SO YOU CAN LEAVE IT.
YOU SHOULDN'T BE RIDING A BIKE.
I'M FINE.
NO, YOU'RE NOT.
YEAH, I WAS PLANNING TO SAY "HI" TOMORROW ...
BESIDES, MY BIKE'S STILL THERE.
YEAH, YOUR PARENTS ARE PRETTY LIBERAL ALSO...
BUT I'M SURE THEY'D PANIC IF THEY SAW YOU LIKE THAT.
WHAT THE HELL...?
HUH? CAN'T I STAY HERE UNTIL THINGS DIE DOWN?
WHAT?!
YOU CAN STAY.
THANKS ♡
HEY...!
WELL, I GOTTA RUN.
YOU'RE LEAVING? WHY DON'T YOU STAY FOR DINNER?
NAH, I'D BETTER GET GOING.
"why don't you stay"? it's my place!!
that's more like it!
OH... HEY, WAIT UP!

HEY.
DING
HERE'S THAT BOOK YOU WANTED TO BORROW.
OH. THANKS.

チン‥
DING
ぐしゃ
RUSTLE
ぐしゃ
RUSTLE
LATER.
YEAH...
THAT KISS TOOK MY BREATH AWAY...
BECAUSE WE WERE IN THE ELEVATOR... RIGHT...?
パタ
STEP
パタ
STEP
HUH? SENSEI...?
!

HEY!
BAM
SENSEI WANTED TO CHANGE THE SHEETS, SO I WAS HELPING HIM.
CAN'T THINK OF A BETTER EXCUSE?
I WAS HOLDING THIS END AND SENSEI TOLD ME TO FLAP IT, AND THEN WE GOT TANGLED UP...
BREAK IT UP
LET ME TELL YOU SOMETHING... IF YOU KEEP HITTING ON SENSEI...
HE'LL PROBABLY DO IT WITH YOU.
PRETTY CONFIDENT THERE...
HEY...!
BUT IT DOESN'T MEAN HE'S GONNA CHOOSE YOU OVER ME!
YOU SURE?
ABSO-LUTELY.
HEY!
I THINK...
CON-FUSED?
HEH
I HAVEN'T HAD *TIME* TO THINK BECAUSE OF YOU...

HAVE YOU BEEN ABLE TO FIGURE OUT WHAT SENSEI REALLY *WANTS?*
HMM... I DON'T THINK *SENSEI* KNOWS WHAT HE WANTS...
...
I'VE ALMOST GIVEN UP TRYING TO FIGURE IT OUT MYSELF...
WHY AM I ASKING *YOU?!* I MUST BE AT AN ALL-TIME LOW!
FWA HA HA HA HA HA
YOU BASTARDS..!
UH-OH.
BUMMER.
GET OUT! BOTH OF YOU!
HERE WE GO AGAIN.
TEMPER, TEMPER.
げしっ げしっ
KICK KICK
バターン
SLAM
WHY'D YOU HAVE TO PISS HIM OFF?
I THINK IT WAS YOU.
NO, IT WAS YOU.

I DON'T THINK SENSEI KNOWS WHAT HE WANTS...

GOING TO BAMBINO'S TONIGHT?

PROBABLY.

I MAY GO WITH KAGAMI TO PICK UP HIS BIKE.

FSHHHH

WHAT'S WRONG?

oh, hey...

THIS? IT'S NOTHING... JUST TOOK AN ELBOW TO THE EYE.

FSHHHHH

LET ME SEE.

HOLY ...!

WHOA! NICE SHINER!

HOW'S YOUR VISION?
IT'S OKAY.
HOW ABOUT HERE?
NAH...
OW...
DOES IT HURT?
HMM... IT LOOKS OKAY, BUT YOU SHOULD GO TO THE NURSE'S OFFICE JUST IN CASE.
OKAY.
CATCH YOU LATER.
I'M STILL...
CONFUSED...
I GUESS...
YEAH.

YUASA ♡
LONG TIME, NO SEE!
YEP. I'M HERE WITH KAGAMI.
I HEARD FROM NAGAI HE'S GONNA BE OKAY?

YEAH...
SO WHERE *IS* YOSHI?
AT THE CORNER BAR.
HE WANTS ME TO WALK OVER *THERE?*
THEY'RE HERE...?
HE MUST BE AFRAID HE'LL GET JUMPED AGAIN.

PSSHT
LIAR.
HEH
HE'S WORRIED IF ANYTHING HAPPENS, THAT CUTIE TEACHER OF YOURS MIGHT GET *HURT*.
SO, IS HE IN LOVE WITH THAT TEACHER?
THE TEACHER WHO I'M LIVING WITH.
oh, my...
...

FORGET THEM. THEY'LL GET THEIRS SOONER OR LATER.
YEAH, BUT SEEING THEM HERE...
PISSES ME OFF.
I CAN'T FORGET KAGAMI, COVERED IN BLOOD...
TO THINK THEY MIGHT HURT HIM, OR SENSEI, OR ANYONE I CARE ABOUT AGAIN...
DOES THAT INCLUDE ME?
OF COURSE!
OH, YOU'RE SO CUTE! I LOVE YOU ♡
BUT... SOMETHING *IS* WRONG WITH YOU TODAY...
LIKE YOU'RE ABOUT TO EXPLODE.
WELL, MY FRIEND JUST ARRIVED, SO...
ガタ
CREAK
OH, HEY... C'MON!
KAGAMI?

TRYING TO AVOID US, EH?
LET'S KICK HIS ASS AGAIN AND MAKE HIM BRING OVER HIS TEACHER!
YEAH, LOOKS LIKE HE CAME TO PICK UP HIS BIKE.
WHERE...? I SEE...
NAH, THAT'S BORING...
MAYBE WE'LL RUN HIM AND HIS BIKE OVER WITH OUR CAR...?
LET ME KNOW WHEN HE'S ABOUT TO LEAVE, OKAY?
heh
SO WHEN SENSEI'S IN-VOLVED, YUASA GOES INTO ACTION? HE COULD'VE JUST GIVEN HIM A CALL...
...I'D BETTER GO WARN HIM.

...
HM?
HUH? KEYS TO THE BIKE? YEAH, YUASA'S GOT THEM.
I JUST GOT A CALL FROM YUASA TELLING ME TO STAY INSIDE...
HUH? I DON'T KNOW... THAT'S ALL HE SAID, THEN HE HUNG UP.
LET ME KNOW WHEN HE'S ABOUT TO LEAVE, OKAY?
WAIT A MINUTE...!
WHAT...?!
RRRRRRRRRRRRRR
RRRRRRRRRRRR
YUASA!
RRRRRRR

WHAT ARE YOU DOING?!
IT'S MY FAULT!
WHAT?!
RRRRRRRRRRRRRRRRR
IF SENSEI HADN'T MET ME, NONE OF THIS WOULD'VE HAPPENED...
RRRR
AND YOU WOULDN'T HAVE BEEN HURT!
RRRR
WHAT THE FUCK...? WHAT HAPPENED TO ME AND SENSEI IS OUR RESPONSIBILITY...!
RRRRRRRR
I WON'T LET IT HAPPEN AGAIN!
VROOM
YUASA!

THERE HE IS!

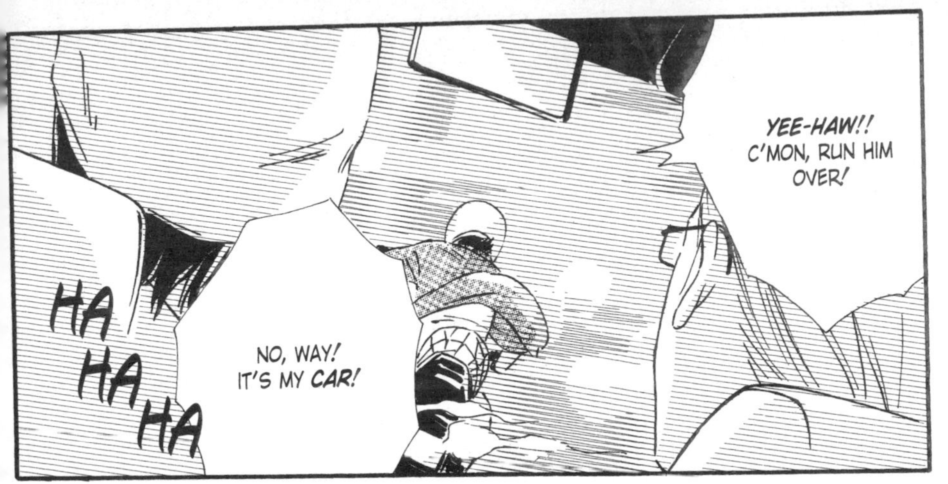

HE'S SPEEDING UP!

DON'T LOSE THAT PRICK!

WHAT THE HELL, MAN...? MOVE OVER!
SLAM
SLAM
SHUT UP! KEEP THOSE ASHES OFF THE CARPET!
DUMBASS! WATCH WHERE YOU'RE GOING...!
OH, SH --
SCREEEEEE
WOOO
WOOO
WOOO

KERCHAK

HAAH HAAH...

SENSEI...

WHAT...
THERE WAS AN ACCIDENT...
HUUH
HUUH
KNOCK
ARE YOU HIS FAMILY?
NO, BUT I CALLED THEM. THEY SHOULD BE HERE SOON.
SHUT
IT DOESN'T LOOK GOOD...
WHAT...?
THEY SAID THEY CAN'T OPERATE ON HIM...
SO...
WHAT... ARE YOU SAYING...?

HUUH
HUUH
HUUH
HUUH
HUUH
HUUH
WHERE ARE THEY?
WHAT?

SENSEI?
ガ
CREAK
THE EYE DROPS.
I KNOW...
YOU'RE NOT THE CRYING TYPE IN ANY SITUATION! C'MON... WHERE ARE THEY?! STOP PLAYING AROUND!
SENSEI!
YUASA! WAKE UP!
SENSEI, CALM DOWN!
BAM
WHAT'S GOING ON IN THERE?!
THIS IS A HOSPITAL!

MURMUR
ザワ
WHAT'S GOING ON?
DOCTOR ...!
ぺこ
BOW
HUUH
HUUH
HUUH
HIS BREATHING IS ABNORMAL BECAUSE OF THE DAMAGE TO HIS LUNGS...
BUT HE'S SEDATED, SO HE SHOULDN'T BE FEELING ANY PAIN...
PLEASE, TRY TO BE CALM FOR HIS SAKE.
...
IS HIS FAMILY HERE?
NO... NOT YET.

I SEE...
PLEASE TELL THEM TO COME SOON...
HUUH
HUUH
HUUH
HUUH
HUUH
HUUH
HUUH
HUUH
YUASA...
HUUH
HUUH

HUUH
HUUH
HUUH
HUUH
HUUH
HUUH
HUUH
HUUH
HUUH
HUUH
HUUH
HUUH
HUUH
HUUH
HUUH
HUUH
HUUH
HUUH
HUUH
HUUH
HUUH
HUUH
HUUH
HUUH
ぱ
BLINK
ち
HWAAAAAAH!

HAAH
HAAH
WHAT THE...?! I COULDN'T BREATHE...
WHAT'S THIS? IS IT PLUGGED IN...?
HEY, SENSEI. WHAT'S UP?
WHAT'S WRONG...?
BAM
バーン
OH.
ずる...
DRAG
WH...WHAT ARE YOU DOING...?!
DRAG
ずる
DRAG
ずる
ずる
DRAG
ずる

THIS IS WHY I DIDN'T WANT TO GO ALONG WITH IT!!
OW! OW!
YANK
ALONG WITH *WHAT?*
I JUST CAN'T SAY "NO" TO YOSHI!!
WHO IS THIS GUY WITH THE *VIOLENT TEMPER?!*
DO YOU KNOW HIM...
yoshi...?
DOCTOR?
SLICK
YES?
IS EVERYTHING ALL RIGHT?
EVERYTHING'S FINE, BUT VISITING HOURS ARE OVER.
...
ONCE HIS FAMILY ARRIVES, WE'LL NEED TO PROCESS HIS INPATIENT PAPERWORK.
yes, sir.
no problem!

I GUESS A NIGHT HERE MAKES ME AN INPATIENT.
ONE NIGHT?
YEAH, IT'S LATE AND I HAVE SOME CHECK-UPS STILL... I SHOULD BE OUT BY TOMORROW.
はっ
FWIP
YOU WEREN'T RUN OVER?!
MINOR SCRAPES
I WAS SAVED, BECAUSE I FELL OFF THE BIKE PROPERLY!
SHEESH
YOU...
TOSS
ポイ
WHAT ARE THOSE?
WHY ARE YOUR EYES RED?
BECAUSE OF HIM.
WHAT?
these are to help you get teary-eyed!
YOINK
とーっ
WHY DON'T YOU DO IT?
EYE POKE
TOSS
ポイ
KEEP THEM.
you may need to cry soon...

SO, IT WAS ALL PART OF YOUR CHARADE?
HUH? OH, COME ON... YUASA WANTED TO KNOW SENSEI'S **TRUE FEELINGS** SO I HELPED HIM OUT...
SINCE IT WAS MY FAULT HE WAS SO CONFUSED.
CREAK
I HAD TO DO **SOMETHING** TO OPEN YOU UP...
BESIDES, IT'S NOT EVERY DAY I GET TO SEE YOU --
SMACK
CAREFUL... THIS IS MY LAST PAIR OF GLASSES.
I HOPE YOU'LL CRY IF IT EVER HAPPENS TO ME.

LATER!
YEAH...
パタン
KACHAK

YOU'RE OKAY LEAVING THEM TOGETHER?

WHAT ABOUT YOU?

MEH... I'LL LET THEM HAVE TONIGHT.

HAVE ***WHAT*** TONIGHT?

I'M MORE INTERESTED IN YOU...

HMM... SENSEI'S MAD AT ME...

CAN I STAY AT YOUR PLACE TONIGHT?

HUH?

BY THE WAY, HOW'S YOUR BIKE?

AH, WHO CARES? AS LONG AS YUASA'S OKAY.

SCRAP METAL.

NO WAY!

MAN, I DON'T UNDERSTAND YOU.

END

SLEEPING BEAUTY
PSHHT

MMN...
むっちりプリン
ピト
TAP
FIRM PUDDING
HEH
すぴ
ZZZ
SNORE

BEEP
BEEP
BEEP
ピッ
BLIP
ぴゅ~
FWOOSH
198 yen.
ピ BLIP
BLIP ピ
538 yen.
314 yen.
ピ BLIP
ピ BLIP
BEEP
BEEP
BEEP
BLIP
BLIP

WOOSH
ぴゅ
thank you!
BEEP
BEEP
BEEP
ピリリ
ピリリ
ピリリ
ピッ
BLIP
タイトル・ガリ勉くん
TITLE: THE HOT NERD
ぴゅ〜
WOOSH

ぜーはー
HUFF PUFF
ぜーはー
WHEEZE WHEEZE
ゴン
BONK
new photo in-progress
MM...
SIGH...

HOW ABOUT THIS?

NAH, IT'S BETTER THIS WAY.

IT'S MORE EROTIC THIS WAY.

...

YEAH, BUT THE ANGLE...

HEY, HOW'S IT GOING?

HUH? HOW'D YOU GET IN?

THE DOOR WAS OPEN.

OH. MUST'VE BEEN ME!

COULDN'T YOU PUT STUFF AWAY FIRST?

ガサ

RUSTLE

...

BEHIND YOU...

END

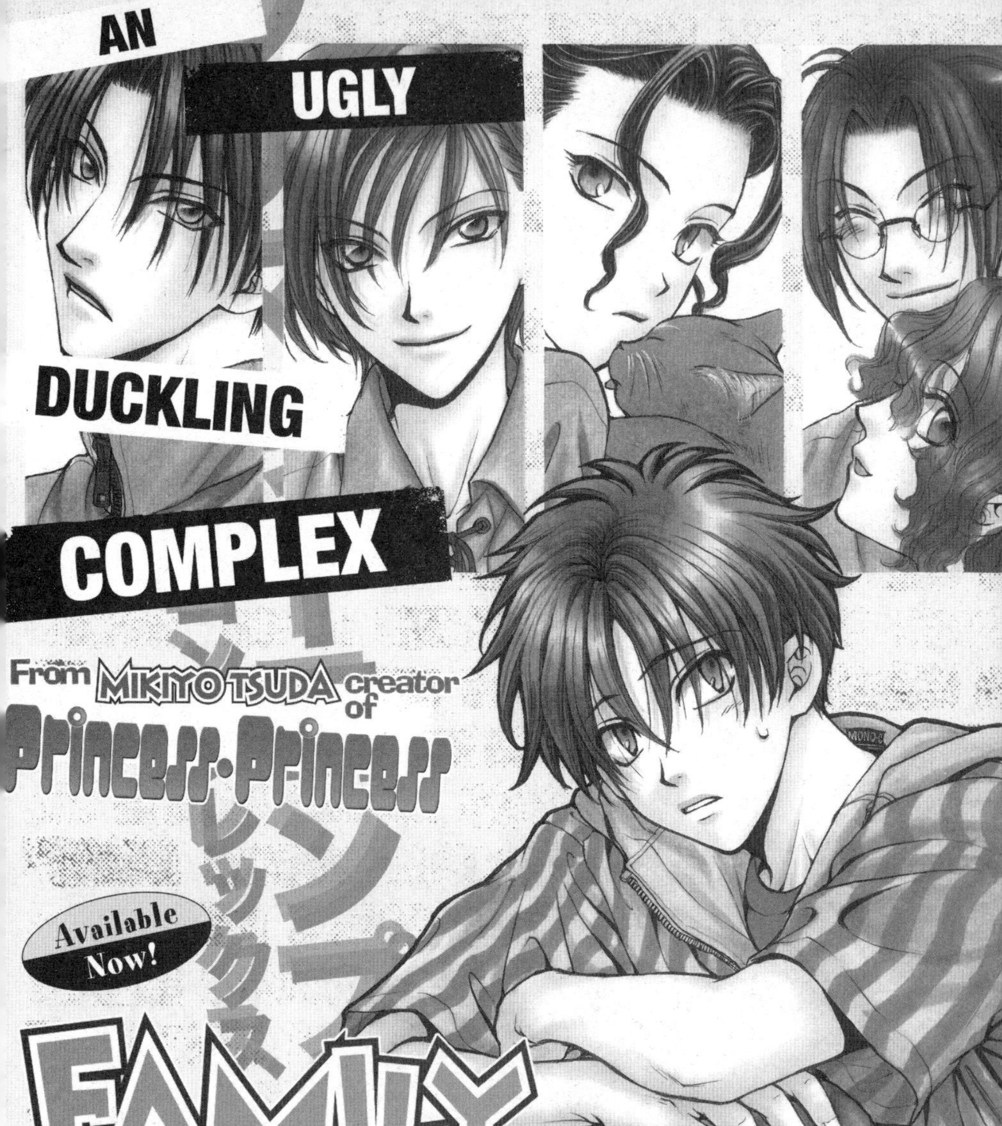
AN
UGLY
DUCKLING
COMPLEX

DMP
DIGITAL MANGA
PUBLISHING

First came
the anime...

This is the back of the book! Start from the other side.

NATIVE MANGA readers read manga from *right to left*.

If you run into our ***Native Manga*** *logo on any of our books... you'll know that this manga is published in it's true original native Japanese right to left reading format, as it was intended. Turn to the other side of the book and start reading from right to left, top to bottom.*

Follow the diagram to see how its done.
Surf's Up!